A HANDBOOK TO THE
PENSION BUILDING

HOME OF THE
NATIONAL BUILDING MUSEUM

Linda Brody Lyons

With a foreword by Brendan Gill

National Building Museum
Washington, DC

We thank the staff, interns, and volunteers whose research over many years has made this book possible.

© 1989 by the National Building Museum

National Building Museum
Judiciary Square, NW
Washington, DC 20001

Printed in the United States of America

Produced by the Publications Office, National Building Museum
Designed by Stephen Kraft
Printed by Peake Printers, Inc., Cheverly, Maryland
Edited by Joyce Elliott

Library of Congress Cataloging-in-Publication Data

Lyons, Linda Brody, 1942–
    A handbook to the Pension Building: home of the National Building Museum / Linda Lyons ; with a foreword by Brendan Gill.
    p. cm.
    ISBN 0-9619752-1-0
    1. National Building Museum (U.S.)   I. Title.
NA6700.W37L96 1989
725' . 12'09753—dc20   89-13097
                                          CIP

Photo Credits   Architect of the Capitol inside cover, p. 11
Terren Baker pp. 1, 31 (middle)
B. Christopher Bene pp. 41 (top), 53
Jack E. Boucher/HABS front cover, pp. 4, 8, 48
Stephen Consiglio pp. 26 (top), 30 (middle), 39, 45, 50, 57 (top right), 62, 64
District of Columbia Public Library p. 57 (middle)
Dunlap Society p. 24 (middle)
George Eisenman/HABS pp. 52 (bottom)
General Accounting Office p. 52 (top)
Gary Griffin pp. 30 (bottom), 36 (top right and bottom), 37, 40 (bottom), 59
Ronnie Haber p. 44 (top and bottom)
F. Harlan Hambright back cover, pp. 18, 28 (bottom right), 29 (top and bottom), 30 (top), 32–33, 35 (top), 42 (top), 61 (bottom)
Harper's Weekly, p. 209, 16 March 1889, p. 17 (top)
Anice Hoachlander p. 31 (bottom)
Library of Congress, Prints and Photographs Division, pp. 20 (middle), 21 (middle left), 36 (top left), 52 (middle), 56 (top and bottom)
Museum of Afro American History, Boston p. 31 (top)
National Archives and Record Administration pp. 7, 14–15, 16 (top and bottom), 20 (top and bottom), 21 (top, middle right, and bottom), 24–25 (top), 27 (bottom right), 28 (bottom left), 34, 41 (bottom), 42 (bottom), 51
National Building Museum pp. 25, 27 (top), 40 (top), 43, 57 (bottom)
Private Collection p. 54
Walter Smalling, Jr. p. 61 (top)
Smithsonian Institution, Engineering Division p. 19
The White House/Michael Sargent p. 57 (top)

Table of Contents

5   Foreword

9   Introduction

10   Beginnings

11   Montgomery C. Meigs, Architect and Engineer

13   The Inventive Design of the Pension Building

19   The Record of Construction

23   Exploring the Pension Building

34   The Interior

51   History in the Pension Building

59   Renovation and Contemporary Use

61   Epilogue

63   Glossary

This publication was made possible with support from The J. M. Kaplan Fund and the Brick Institute of America.

Foreword

Of the many ways of recounting the history of a country, not the least interesting is through a description of its architecture. In his poem, "The Gift Outright," Robert Frost has written of the United States, "The land was ours before we were the land's." Which is a way of saying, however indirectly, that the first settlers on the North American continent brought along with them, among other items in their cultural baggage, an architecture appropriate to the landscape and climates of the Old World and yet one that might well prove unsuitable to the very different landscapes and climates of the New. And so it befell, but no matter; little by little, our polyglot ancestors accommodated themselves as builders to circumstances that were nearly always novel to them and often inimical: the fierce snows of New England, the burning suns of the Arizona desert, the rainy benignities of the Pacific Northwest.

When we speak of American architecture, we do well to remind ourselves that throughout most of our history—and even today—the term refers to the so-called built environment as a whole and not to the very small number of structures that are the handiwork of professional architects. Indeed, in the eighteenth century there were many gentleman architects (Washington and Jefferson among them) but few professionals besides Latrobe and Bulfinch. In the nineteenth century, and not without reason, it became a common practice for carpenter-builders to assume the grander title of architect; by dint of self-appointment, lo and behold! they *were* architects. Around the same time, practitioners of the emerging profession of civil engineering extended their efforts beyond battlements, bridges, aqueducts, and the like to such workaday government buildings as customs and court houses.

A few of the structures that have come down to us during the past couple of centuries and that by their presence silently enhance our lives may be famous for their beauty; most of them will be but the unremarked anonymous architecture of city streets, of factories, of country barns, and churches. It is largely in this vernacular architecture that the history of America may be read, manifesting as it does the skills of a hundred disparate occupations: masons, carpenters, plumbers, electricians, metal-workers, roofers, and painters.

The precious physical evidence of the skills of such artisans lies all about us, though we are rarely conscious of it unless some particular structure, defined by scholars as a significant embodiment of our architectural heritage, is said to be in jeopardy. At the moment, many of us are ready to leap upon the barricades in its defense. An admirable gesture, but equally important to us in the long run are the structures that no scholar troubles to call the world's attention to and that may have survived not because they were important but, on the contrary, because they were unimportant. These are the structures out of which the fabric of our towns and cities is woven and from which we draw much emotional nourishment unawares. Humble as they are, they deserve to be cherished and preserved, and yet it happens that they were never in graver peril than today.

For it is the case at present that large portions of our cities are being knocked down and rebuilt, sometimes in the doubtful name of urban renewal but more often thanks to the simple cupidity of real-estate developers. A veritable army of young architects, artisans, and architectural historians must be trained to identify, restore, and (in many cases) devise new uses for the most valuable specimens of our architectural heritage.

Plainly, this is the time for a museum devoted to the recognition and celebration of American building to make itself known—to utter a Whitmanesque yawp over the rooftops of the world. And where better to do so than in a building (ancient by American standards, noble by any standards, and once threatened with demolition) which is itself an exceptionally fine example of what architectural preservationists call adaptive reuse? The history of the Pension Building amounts to an instructive chapter in the history of the United States. Every word of the following account is as well worth reading as every one of the building's 15,500,000 red bricks is worth preserving.

Brendan Gill

Mr. Gill, noted author, architectural critic, and columnist for the *New Yorker*, recently published a biography of Frank Lloyd Wright. He is a trustee of the National Building Museum.

U. S. PENSION BUREAU.

The largest brick building in the world; being composed of fifteen million, five hundred thousand bricks. Cost of building when completed. $900,000.

EXTERIOR DIMENSIONS.

Length, - - - 400 feet.
Width, - - - 200 "

INTERIOR DIMENSIONS OF COURT.

Length, - - - 316 feet.
Width, - - - 116 "
Height, - - - 159 "

Height of each roof-supporting column, 89 feet circumference of each roof-supporting column, 25 feet, and the number of bricks in each column, 100,000.

This early handbill celebrates the impressive dimensions of the Pension Building, albeit with some exaggerations.

Introduction

This small handbook to the Pension Building was truly born of popular demand. So many visitors to the museum concluded their visits with a plea for some remembrance to take with them that we have been obliged, quite happily, to comply with their wishes.

First we asked some questions, better to understand what was desired. The answers provided a fitting testament to the diverse qualities of this remarkable structure. Some visitors wished to recall that first moment of experiencing the majesty and dignity of the Great Hall. Others were intrigued by the technology of the roof trusses and ventilating system. Still others were impressed by the meticulous craftsmanship so evident in the brickwork and decorative details of both interior and exterior.

And most registered an element of surprise. They had not ventured before to this part of town, or if so, had no cause to enter the building (of which the facade, however elegant, gives little hint of what lies inside). This circumstance was easily understood. For, from bright beginnings, the building had fallen over the years into neglect and obscurity. The surrounding neighborhood, once at the vital heart of the capital city, became a depressed backwater as government and commercial activity moved west.

But all of that has changed. Thanks to the wisdom of the Congress and federal government—urged on by a band of thoughtful citizens—the building has been magnificently restored and renovated to become the home, quite appropriately, of a museum celebrating American achievements in the building arts. And the neighborhood is thriving once more as the surrounding blocks have become the site of a redevelopment boom.

Today, the Pension Building endures, not just as an architectural and engineering landmark, but as an embodiment of American craftsmanship and a constant reminder that we must all be ever vigilant to defend and promote the quality of our built environment.

Robert W. Duemling

Mr. Duemling is the President and Director of the National Building Museum.

Beginnings

The Pension Building was built to serve the needs of the Pension Bureau, once a large and important agency of the U. S. Department of the Interior. Created by an act of Congress as the United States Pension Office in 1792, the bureau provided pensions to veterans disabled during the Revolutionary War and to dependent survivors of those who had died in military service. As the years passed, subsequent military conflicts, such as the War of 1812, the Mexican War, and the Civil War, increased the number of pension recipients, causing the bureau to expand into rented buildings around Washington. In addition to this steady growth, the Arrears Act of January 1879 unleashed a flood of new claims.

Finally, in 1881, Congress acknowledged the bureau's pressing need for more space and responded to its urgent request for a central facility. General Montgomery C. Meigs, Quartermaster General of the United States Army, was instructed to find a suitable site and construct a fireproof building for the Pension Bureau at a cost of $250,000 to $300,000. Meigs found a site and created a plan. Ground was broken in 1882, and the Pension Building was first occupied by the bureau in 1884. Construction was completed in 1887.

The Pension Bureau remained in the building until 1926, when it became part of the Veteran's Administration. The General Accounting Office then occupied the building until 1950, followed by numerous government agencies and the District of Columbia Courts. However, the building had become increasingly obsolete as a structure to house modern offices. First threatened by demolition, but saved by historic preservationists, the Pension Building was designated by act of Congress in 1980 as the site of a new museum to celebrate American achievements in the building arts.

Montgomery C. Meigs.

Montgomery C. Meigs, Architect and Engineer

The designer of the Pension Building, General Montgomery Cunningham Meigs (1816–1892), attended the U. S. Military Academy at West Point where he studied both engineering and architectural design, graduating fifth in his class in 1836. After graduation he joined the Army Corps of Engineers and was assigned to assist Lt. Robert E. Lee in surveying the Mississippi River valley.

Meigs became assistant to the chief of the Corps of Engineers, moved to Washington, and in 1853 took charge of constructing an aqueduct to supply the city with water. As part of this project, he designed and built the Cabin John Bridge, 220 feet in length, the longest masonry arch in the world until the twentieth century. A second bridge, over Rock Creek, incorporated massive hollow cast-iron tubes that served both as water supply mains and supporting arches for the bridge. Both bridges combined the dual functions of road and aqueduct in one structure, thus demonstrating Meigs's practical as well as comprehensive approach to design.

Meigs was appointed supervising engineer for the extension of the U. S. Capitol building when Thomas U. Walter, the architect selected for the job, became enmeshed in scandals over the awarding of contracts. Meigs made significant alterations to the plan, such as moving the House and Senate chambers to the centers of their respective wings and surrounding them with corridors to achieve more efficient use of space. He solved heating and ventilating problems and designed a special crane that made construction of the great cast-iron dome possible. He also concerned himself with the decoration of the Capitol, commissioning works of art and hiring artists. However, his enthusiastic supervision of the job and his constant changing of Walter's plans led to a bitter clash between the two men, and he was removed from the Capitol project and "banished" to Florida to fortify Fort Jefferson in the Dry Tortugas.

The threat of Civil War shortened Meigs's exile, and he was recalled to Washington in February 1861. By the end of that year he had been appointed Quartermaster General of the Army through the influence of friends in Congress and on his reputation as a strong administrator. Throughout the war, he effectively managed support for almost a million troops. Of particular note, he constructed a large number of barracks, supply depots, and other functional buildings that were inexpensive, efficient, and quickly built.

In 1867 Meigs toured Europe to recover from years of strenuous work and grief over the death of a son in the war. This trip and another in 1876 provided the opportunity to study Italian Renaissance architecture firsthand. The experience influenced his later architectural designs, especially that of the Pension Building. Like other designers of the nineteenth century, he recognized that Renaissance forms could be readily adapted to meet the needs of new building types and programs.

In 1879 Meigs received the appointment of consulting engineer to supervise the construction of the National Museum building of the Smithsonian Institution (now the Arts and Industries Building). This functional brick and iron fireproof building, completed in 1881, was the least expensive government building yet built, and it influenced the design and construction of federal buildings for several decades. The result was that Meigs's reputation as a builder was greatly enhanced by the success of this project.

On the eve of his retirement as Quartermaster General in 1881, Meigs was appointed by the Senate Appropriations Committee to design for the Pension Bureau a "fireproof building of brick and metal," similar to the National Museum building. The Pension Building was Meigs's last and most important architectural work and the one of which he was most proud. It is noteworthy that in the construction of this building he was listed as both architect and engineer.

This combined responsibility was relatively rare, evoking comment in an 1887 article which Meigs pasted into his scrapbook: "The pension building has been managed in a way very different from that generally followed with government buildings, and an army engineer, officiating as an architect, has produced a building the like of which is not to be seen anywhere else in the country."

The Inventive Design of the Pension Building

As General Meigs planned the "New Pension Office," he had several important goals in mind. His initial instructions from Congress called for a fireproof building to be built on a tight budget. The use of brick for the structure would serve both of these purposes, since this material was the most reliable form of fireproof construction at that time, and locally made brick was relatively inexpensive and readily available. Combustible materials such as wood were avoided where possible, although Meigs did eventually choose to install wooden floors in the offices and a wooden cornice at the roofline. Although metals, such as cast and wrought iron, were considered to be suitable fireproof construction materials, Meigs was concerned about failures that had occurred in earlier fires, as at the nearby Patent Office a decade earlier. He therefore sought to avoid using metal for stairs and major structural elements. He also avoided expensive building materials such as carved stone or fine marble, choosing instead factory-made cast terra cotta or painted plaster on brick surfaces.

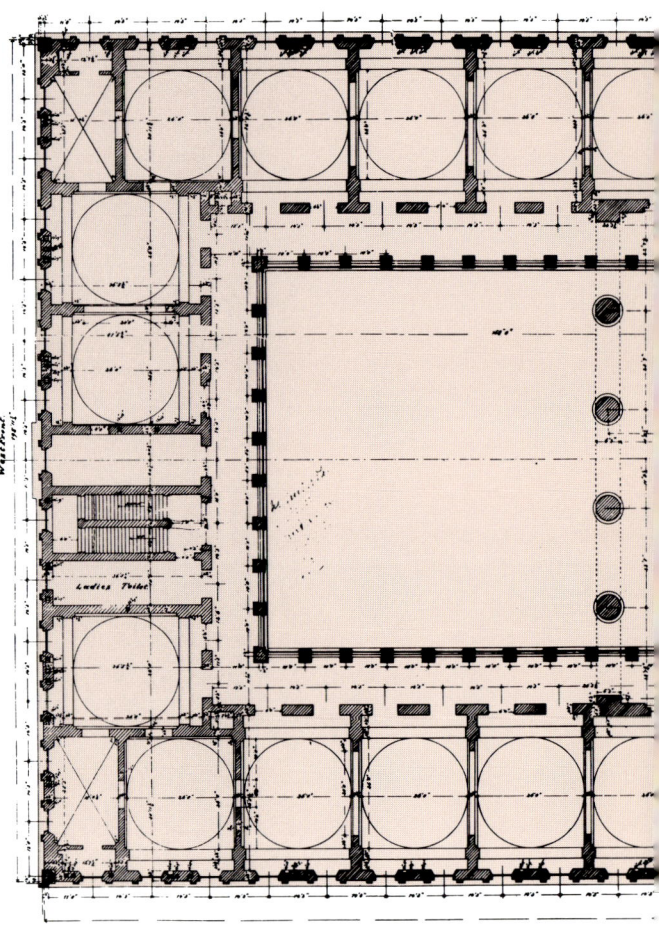

The first-floor plan of 1883 presents in detail such information as the arrangement of offices around the central Great Hall, placement of stairways and utilities, and designation of the types of vaulted ceilings to be constructed in the office spaces.

Meigs expressed a desire to produce a modern and healthful environment for the clerks of the Pension Bureau, and the result is apparent in his careful attention to light and ventilation in the design of the building. The typical office building of the day, government or private, was not considered a healthy or attractive place to work. Dark stuffy rooms, lit by gaslight if at all, were reached by long dark corridors with no sources of ventilation. Disease was thought to thrive in these spaces, especially in a city like Washington, a poorly drained area with long hot summers and damp chilly winters. With this in mind, Meigs turned to the traditional Renaissance plan he had admired in Italy. He placed all of the offices of the Pension Building around the perimeter of a large central Great Hall where they would be exposed to daylight and fresh air from both the exterior of the building and the Great Hall itself. He designed two levels of open arcaded galleries to serve as corridors to the offices.

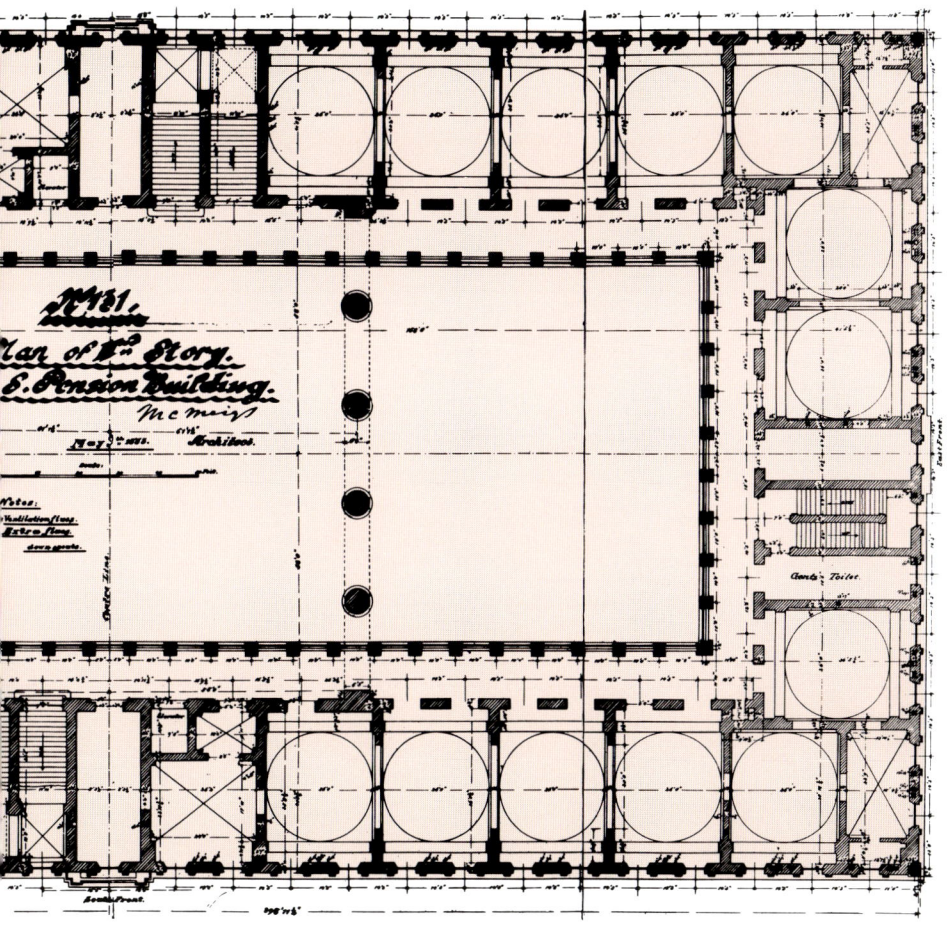

Meigs's innovative plan included no doors to separate offices from the Great Hall or each other. Fresh air would enter the offices from the exterior through large windows, pass over the clerks at their desks, and enter the Great Hall. Now slightly heated, the air would rise and exit the building through the first row of operable clerestory windows. This carefully planned flow of air had the effect of a chimney, pulling more air into the building to create a continuous change of fresh air throughout. In 1885 Meigs reported that under maximal conditions, the volume of air in the Great Hall was replaced every two minutes, a fact which surprised even him. Fresh air could also enter the building through a series of air vents visible as three missing bricks under each window on the exterior of the building. These were particularly intended to provide ventilation during the colder months when windows were closed and were situated behind the steam radiators of each office so that the fresh air could be warmed to room temperature.

Meigs's early interior sketches for the Great Hall show his initial plan to use arcaded galleries as corridors to the perimeter offices, high clerestory windows for ventilation, and dividing screens of colossal columns to support a heavy central roof (later redesigned).

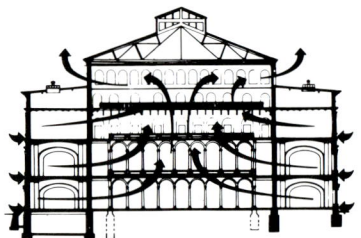

Meigs intended that fresh air enter the building through the office windows and stale air exit through the clerestory.

Other goals that Meigs sought to address included answering the city's need for a large space in which to hold important gatherings and events. The spectacular debut of this space occurred when it was decided to hold Grover Cleveland's 1885 inaugural ball in the Pension Building before construction was completed, thus requiring a temporary wooden roof. The glittering event began a tradition of inaugural balls in the Great Hall that, although interrupted for a time, continues to the present day. Meigs also hoped the Pension Bureau would use the Great Hall as an indoor garden, with large trees and plants placed around the central fountain and throughout the hall. Meigs suggested that the space could be used as a sort of "banking hall" where the bureau could conduct some of its business, although it is doubtful that he would have approved of the office cubicles that were installed in the early-to-mid twentieth century.

Throughout the process of design and construction, Meigs supplemented traditional methods with modern technology to solve problems and achieve building efficiency. He used advanced techniques in the construction of the roof with its supporting trusses of iron and steel. He provided such un-

This 1882 drawing from Meigs's office shows the path of fresh air through vents under each window and into adjustable wooden valves in the sills. The air in the vents was heated as it passed just behind steam radiators in front of each window.

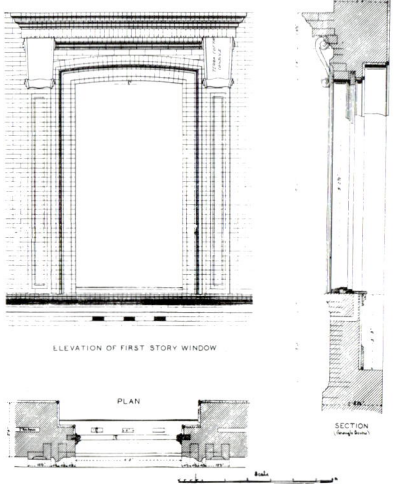

An early inaugural ball, one of the first to be held in the Pension Building.

usual conveniences as document tracks for transporting the Pension Bureau's mass of records throughout the building and intended to equip the building with elevators and electric lights, but these were not approved by Congress at that time, probably for reasons of expense.

Typical of designers in the nineteenth century, Meigs paid as much attention to the appearance of the building as he did to its functional program. He sought to follow the examples of the "best buildings for habitation and for public business in Rome," in particular the most admired Italian Renaissance masterpieces. The exterior of the Pension Building is modeled closely on the sixteenth-century Palazzo Farnese which he had seen on two trips abroad and studied carefully in books devoted to Italian Renaissance architecture. The arcaded galleries that surround the Great Hall echo those of the Cancelleria, much admired for its fine proportions. The colossal Corinthian columns that divide the Great Hall into three bays were inspired, according to Meigs, by similar columns in the church of Santa Maria degli Angeli, also in Rome. Meigs chose Renaissance classicism as his primary vocabulary, one that was becoming increasingly inter-

Palazzo Farnese, Rome, the Italian Renaissance model for the Pension Building facade.

The Great Hall as redecorated in 1984 to evoke its original nineteenth-century appearance.

esting to leading architects of this period. However, his willingness to include a Parthenon-inspired frieze, colossal Roman columns, and a factory-like roof of contemporary design ultimately make the Pension Building a superb example of nineteenth-century eclecticism.

Although he did not have the opportunity to decorate or paint much of the interior of the building, it is clear that Meigs intended to finish the work with an elaborate scheme. The painted ceiling and elegant fireplace that remain in the Pension Commissioner's Suite are good examples. In the Great Hall, Meigs supervised the painting of the roof and the colorful schemes in the lanterns of the east and west bays. He began to bronze the Ionic columns of the arcaded galleries, and it is known that he intended to paint the colossal Corinthian columns with the warm golden tones of Siena marble and bronze their capitals. The fourth-floor balcony was also bronzed.

The Record of Construction

Meigs's initial plans were approved on November 1, 1882, by M.L. Joslyn, Acting Secretary of the Interior, and Robert Todd Lincoln, Secretary of War.

Meigs began work on the new Pension Office by searching for a suitable site. After rejecting two others, he selected one at the north end of Judiciary Square. Preliminary planning for the building itself had begun in 1881, with the final dimensions of 200 by 400 feet decided upon in 1882, and general plans (including a rather detailed rendition of the proposed exterior design) approved by the Secretaries of War and Interior on 1 November 1882. Ground was broken the next day.

Excavation proceeded during the winter and spring, and construction of the cellar and foundation walls began as soon as the weather permitted. In his annual report of September 1883, Meigs stated that the foundation was com-

Construction progress photograph, August 31, 1883.

Meigs ordered photographs to document the progress of construction.

October 4, 1883
Note the slender scaffolding for construction of the colossal columns.

November 1, 1883
Huge piles of bricks fill the worksite.

December 10, 1883
Cast-iron Ionic columns are in place on the second floor.

Probably December 1883
Installation of the frieze was an integral part of construction.

July 2, 1884

Second-floor walls and archways are under construction.

November 14, 1885
Garlands from the
inaugural ball
remain on the
great columns.

November 14, 1885
The exterior is virtually
completed and much
of the building occupied
(note awnings),
but inside work
remains to be done.

pleted, including a vaulted cellar on the south side of the building which had become necessary when the site was found to have been partially filled at an earlier time. The walls of the building had reached the second floor, part of the frieze of Civil War soldiers and sailors was in place, and the bases of the colossal columns built.

As construction proceeded, a number of unanticipated expenses were incurred, and several new appropriations were made that more than doubled the original budget for the building. These covered the problems with the site, the need for thicker walls than anticipated to support the weight of the roof, and higher prices for materials.

The October 1884 annual report announced that the exterior walls, perimeter offices, and arcaded galleries were built to the level of the third story; the masonry of the great columns was complete with two of the Corinthian capitals in place; the ironwork for the roof had been ordered; heating and plumbing installation was continuing; and most of the terracotta elements had been delivered and paid for. Also in this report Meigs brought up the idea, which he had previously considered, of adding a fourth floor to the building. Since the design of the exterior required a tall third story, its thirty-one-foot height left ample room for another floor. Meigs proposed to insert a brick vaulted ceiling on rolled-iron beams nineteen feet above the third floor to provide support for thirty-six additional rooms for storage of pension records.

By March 1885 the perimeter rooms had been roofed, and shortly after Cleveland's inaugural ball the Pension Bureau, following a pioneer contingent that had arrived in 1884, began to move into the unfinished building, achieving full occupancy by the end of the year. In his construction report of September 1885, Meigs stated that all office rooms were glazed and most occupied; steam boilers, pipes, and most radiators were functioning; the two ends of the Great Hall were roofed; and five of the nine iron trusses of the central pavilion roof were in place. He proposed using electric lights, which had been a great success at the inaugural ball, to light the Great Hall at night.

Meigs's September 1886 report found the roof and masonry completed and the clerestory glazed to enclose the building completely, work on the Great Hall floor beginning, plastering, brickwork for the fourth floor, and the upper flights of stairs in progress. He noted with pride that time lost by sickness among bureau employees was reduced by 8,622 days in one year in the new building.

In his September 1887 report, Meigs recorded the completion of most of the building and made requests for items that had not been funded previously or repairs that were already necessary. He went on to describe the efficiency and function of the building and summarized its cost. During five years of painstaking supervision, Meigs had built the largest brick building in the world, containing 15,500,000 bricks at a total expenditure of $886,614.04. As he stated in the report, "The building is now substantially completed. It has been occupied for over two years in an unfinished condition; the hall not plastered and not paved. Those who live in it appear to be content with it and I believe that its continued use will justify the theory of its design and construction."

Exploring the Pension Building

Foundation

The foundation of the Pension Building is stuccoed rubble stone walls about four feet thick supported by concrete footings about six feet wide and three feet deep. The colossal columns of the Great Hall rest on individual thirteen-foot-square concrete footings. There is a basement under the south half of the building which had not been planned originally but became necessary when the ground under that part of the site was found to have been previously filled.

Walls

The exterior walls are load-bearing and of brick masonry construction, seventy-five feet high and two feet four inches thick, composed of common brick faced with pressed brick, decorative brick, and ornamental terra cotta. The Pension Building represents a relatively early use of ornamental terra cotta, as a less-expensive substitute for carved stone or iron. The pressed brick is laid in running bond with narrow joints tinted to match, giving the effect of a smooth continuous surface. Meigs decided to hire bricklayers directly because his experience had shown that the quality of workmanship he desired was not available through public contractors. To find qualified workers he advertised as far away as Baltimore and Philadelphia. Although the building had no cornerstone, a brief ceremony took place in which a handful of coins amounting to thirty-one cents was placed under the first pressed brick to be laid on the exterior.

The exterior elevation approved in 1882 has an early roof design that was later changed to a simpler plan, probably for reasons of cost. The rest of the design was built as planned. Note the unusual circular brick and terra-cotta columns set into the corners of the upper two floors.

Traditionally, the east and west entrances are thought to symbolize war (above), having a male mask on the

The design of the exterior, combining pedimented windows, frieze, belt courses, and a cornice in the Italian Renaissance style, is derived primarily from the Palazzo Farnese in Rome, although Meigs modified the details to introduce a military theme. However, unlike the Palazzo which is square, the Pension Building is a large rectangle. There are twenty-seven window bays on the north and south facades, while the east and west facades have thirteen. Each facade has an entrance in the center. Meigs arrived at this design very early in his planning of the building, and the exterior walls and cornice seen today are essentially those of the first approved plan of 1882.

Entrances

The entrances, called gateways or gates by Meigs, are defined by projecting brick archways. Above each the main frieze of Civil War soldiers and sailors presents a military unit that defines the theme of the entrance. The archways are also adorned with terra-cotta relief spandrels and decorative key-

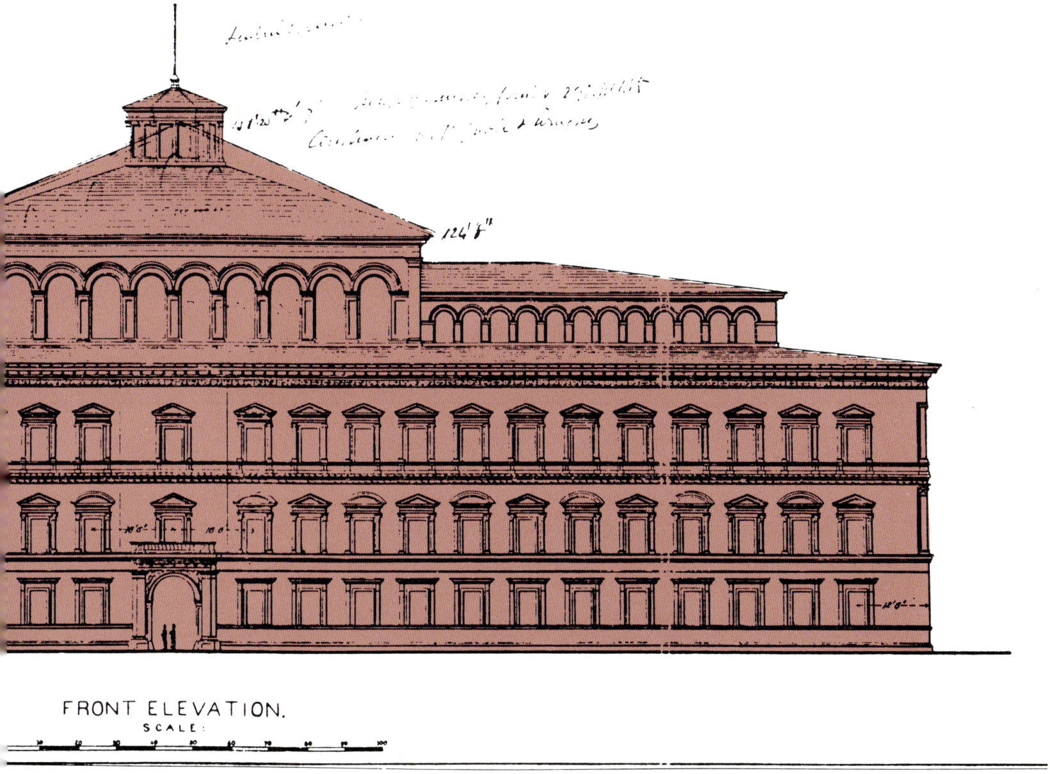

FRONT ELEVATION.
SCALE:

keystone and the figures of Minerva and Mars, the goddess and god of War, in the left and right spandrels. The north and south entrances appear to symbolize peace (right), having a female mask on the keystone and in the spandrels the allegorical figures of truth or liberty on the left and justice on the right.

The entrances are also distinguished from each other by the military unit in the main frieze of Civil War soldiers and sailors that is featured above each: the Gate of the Quartermaster on the west (left, before cleaning and installation of new doors), the Gate of the Infantry on the South (right), the Naval Gate on the east, and the Gate of the Invalids on the north.

stones. Within the north, south, and west entrances were pairs of wood-and-glass panel doors flanked by narrow sidelights which are now replaced by modern firesafe doors of full width in a similar design. The wood-and-glass transoms above these doors and those of the east service entrance are original.

Frieze

The most outstanding decorative feature of the facade is the continuous belt course, or frieze, of buff-colored terra cotta between the first and second levels. This low relief was designed by Caspar Buberl (1834–1899), a Bohemian-born

> A.D. 1883. PRESIDENT OF THE UNITED STATES CHESTER A. ARTHUR. VICE PRESIDENT. GEO. F. EDMUNDS. SPEAKER OF THE HOUSE OF REPRESENTATIVES J. WARREN KEIFER. SECRETARY OF THE INTERIOR HENRY M. TELLER. COMMISSIONER OF PENSIONS WILLIAM W. DUDLEY. POPULATION OF THE UNITED STATES. 54 2/2738. REVENUE OF THE UNITED STATES. 398287582. DOLS. APPROPRIATION FOR MILITARY AND NAVAL PENSIONS. 99 460 000. DOLS. NEW PENSION OFFICE. ARCHITECT. GEN. MONTGOMERY. C. MEIGS. U.S.A.

The marble plaque on the south entrance wall may have commemorated an important visit to or approval of the building early in its construction. An interesting feature of the plaque is the information it provides about the importance of the Pension Bureau at that time. The 1883 revenues of the United States were $398,287,582, while the expenditures for military and naval pensions were $99,460,-000, almost one quarter of the country's revenues. The plaque also carries a curious error: George F. Edmunds is listed as Vice President of the United States, but he was in fact President Pro Tempore of the Senate, next in line to succeed President Chester Arthur who had succeeded James Garfield upon the latter's death in 1881.

sculptor who at that time was much admired and a recipient of major commissions for public sculpture. Three feet high and 1,200 feet long, the frieze is composed of individual panels of varying length displaying Civil War forces—a continuous parade of Union infantry, cavalry, artillery, navy, quartermaster, and medical units.

In the process of developing the building design, Meigs first requested models from the Boston Terra Cotta Company, the primary source of terra cotta for the building, providing them with a list of potential subjects. He was not pleased with what they sent, so then sought the services of Buberl, with whose work he had become acquainted at the Smithsonian's National Museum building. Buberl first created each design in clay. He then made a plaster cast of each, which he sent from his studio to the Boston Terra Cotta Company. From this plaster cast, a repeat plaster mold was produced into which the terra cotta was pressed to make a sufficient number of clay casts for a total of 1,200 feet around the building. The twenty-eight individual panels, from two to four feet in length, representing sixty-nine and one-half linear feet of original designs, are repeated in varying order along the length of the frieze.

The famous frieze of the Parthenon was the prototype for the Pension Building frieze. Meigs and Buberl corresponded on such subjects as the procession of "pedestrian figures followed by the youths of Athens on horseback." Meigs was also familiar with the contemporary work of Eadweard Muybridge (1830–1904), the photographer who pioneered in studies of animals in motion, and he sent a book by Muybridge, as well as one on military uniforms, to Buberl. The result of this attention to detail on the part of both architect and sculptor is seen throughout the frieze. It is a dra-

One of the most dramatic aspects of Meigs's difficulties with the cornice concerns the more than 400 terra-cotta lions' heads produced from a bold design of Caspar Buberl. Several had fallen off, and Meigs ordered the remainder removed to prevent further accidents. He concluded that the hollow forms were accumulating water in their interiors which then froze and expanded to crack the terra cotta, and he began to consider interior uses. Only one head remains in the building today, just below the fourth-floor balcony soffit on the south wall of the Great Hall.

These drawings, one from the widely read nineteenth-century study of Roman buildings by Letarouilly (right), and one from Meigs's office (left), show that although Meigs was copying the cornice of the Palazzo Farnese to an exacting standard, he nevertheless adapted the decorative details to reflect a military theme.

To echo the repeating rhythm of alternating fleurs-de-lis and acanthus leaves, he created a band of stylized cannons and bursting bombs. A similar effect was achieved on a smaller band above the second-floor windows (see photograph on page 30) in which crossed swords alternate with sets of cannon balls, chains, and stars.

matic three-dimensional pictorial procession as well as an accurate and realistic depiction of uniformed men and animals in motion.

Cornice

In planning the exterior cornice, in his first approved plan of 1882, Meigs carefully imitated the design of the Palazzo Farnese, and, having closely followed that model, he did not alter his plan. This was not true, however, of the details of its construction. Although Meigs originally intended the cornice to be made of iron, after further study he selected terra cotta, convinced that it could be made light and strong and at less cost. Later, however, he abandoned the all-terra-cotta cornice for one of wood with terra-cotta ornamentation. Once the terra-cotta modillions were in place, work began on the wooden eave trough, to be lined with copper. Terra-cotta rosettes were attached to the underside of the trough between the modillions, and terra-cotta lions' heads were placed on the cavetto or curved portion of the cornice.

The use of wood drew criticism from several sources concerned about fireproof construction and the safety of attaching heavy terra-cotta ornament to a material that would rot and create the danger of falling pieces. Meigs vigorously defended his choices, but, in fact, he experienced difficulties almost immediately in working with the two essentially incompatible materials. In the long run, there were always problems with deterioration of wood cornice elements and serious structural problems with the terra-cotta modillions that have only recently been corrected. The terra-cotta lions' heads and rosettes had to be removed and have never been replaced on the exterior of the building.

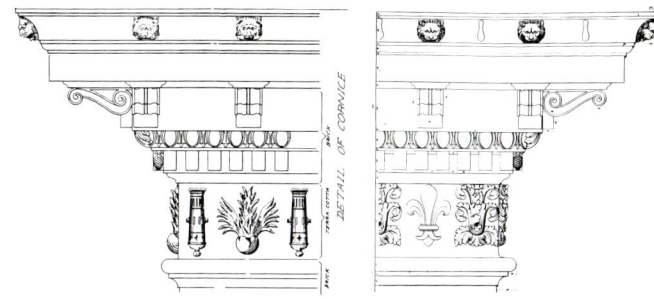

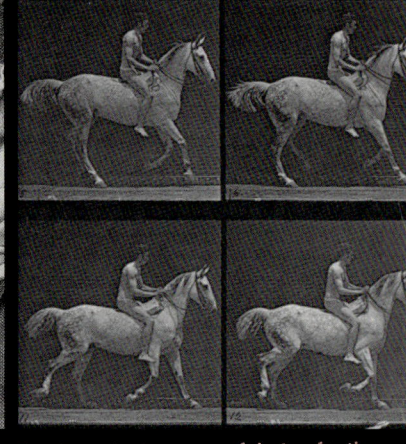

Two important sources of design for the Pension Building's frieze were the ancient frieze of the Parthenon (left) and nineteenth century photographic studies of motion by Eadweard Muybridge (right).

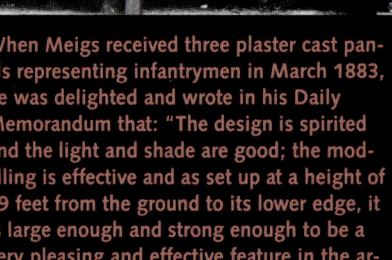

When Meigs received three plaster cast panels representing infantrymen in March 1883, he was delighted and wrote in his Daily Memorandum that: "The design is spirited and the light and shade are good; the modelling is effective and as set up at a height of 19 feet from the ground to its lower edge, it is large enough and strong enough to be a very pleasing and effective feature in the architecture of such a building."

The use of molded terra cotta allowed the manufacturer to increase the variety of images depicted in the frieze by removing parts of the original composition before firing the clay. This photograph shows a group of infantry soldiers that was altered by removing one of the figures. Other examples can be found throughout the frieze.

Although the frieze is often thought to be a commissioned monument or memorial, there was no federal legislation that designated either building or frieze as such. Meigs wrote in his 1883 Annual Report that: "[the] frieze alludes to the origin of the Bureau for whose use the building is intended."

The pedimented windows, richly ornamented in decorative brick and terra cotta, are separated by belt courses and vary on each level according to Renaissance practice. On the first level, flat molded lintels supported by consoles rest on paneled pilasters (bottom photograph and drawing on page 16). The second-floor windows, flanked by pilasters with Ionic capitals, are arranged in a pattern of alternating curved and triangular pediments (top photograph before installation of new windows). At the third-floor, Corinthian pilasters support triangular pediments and rest on double consoles contained within a paneled belt course.

Working on the roof in 1986 during renovation of the building. Note the plain bricks and standard mortar of the clerestory wall.

Clerestory Walls

Above the cornice, the clerestory walls are not as elaborate as the walls below. Meigs felt he could save on materials in this area because it would be hidden from view by the lower roof, unless the viewer was standing quite far away. The arcaded clerestory walls are faced with inexpensive common red brick set in standard mortar. The architectural details are rendered by corbelling standard bricks rather than using custom-made molded brick.

Roof

While the base of the Pension Building was modeled on the Palazzo Farnese, Meigs did not have a Renaissance model for the roof, for the technology needed to roof such great spaces with iron and steel trusses had appeared only in the last few decades. Meigs wrote in his report of October 1881 that the latest improvements in technology "have made possible the addition of durable and safe roofs of large span covering central courtyards and making their whole space available for office purposes as well as for ventilation of the building."

The roof design that was finally executed seems in its simplicity to have been dictated by financial necessity. The upper portion consists of a tall, central gable roof perpendicular to the main axis of the building and two lower gable roofs on either side parallel to the main axis. Lanterns thirty-two by seventy-four feet were added on top of the side roofs to admit more light and improve ventilation through operable double-glazed windows. Visible on the lower perimeter roof are the skylights provided to light and ventilate the fourth-floor storage rooms. The skylights in place now are reproductions of the original ones which were carefully planned with vertical glass to reduce heat buildup in summer.

The roof was built in three stages, first over the perimeter offices, then the side bays of the central Great Hall, and finally the center of the Great Hall. The roof of the Great Hall is supported by trusses of wrought iron and steel. It was originally composed of terra-cotta tiles covered with tarred paper and tin sheathing. Meigs's first choice for the latter would have been copper, but the need for economy prevailed.

Although Meigs took great care in designing and constructing the roof and making it fireproof, it was never fully waterproof—to the detriment of pension records. Even before the building was finished, the perimeter roof over the offices was damaged by falling bricks and snow and the movement of workmen. Meigs rectified this by installing a second layer of tiles topped with wood planking which also protected the roof from damage caused by men walking on it to open and close the clerestory windows. In subsequent years the roof has been replaced several times. The current roof consists of precast concrete tiles and terne-coated stainless steel painted the color of oxidized copper.

Two chimneys appear on the southwest portion of the building. The large chimney, which extends forty-four feet above the level of the lower roof, served the basement boiler room for the steam heating system. It is constructed of common brick and embellished with terra-cotta belt courses and a plaque of a mounted infantry officer. The smaller chimney serves the fireplace in the second-floor Pension Commissioner's Suite.

The main chimney was once embellished by a special feature that perfectly illustrated Meigs's nineteenth-century enthusiasm for classical ornament. This was a cap made of a large sugar pan supported by three cast-iron legs in the form of Rocky Mountain sheep, created for Meigs by Caspar Buberl.

New skylights, reproductions of the original designs, were installed in 1987.

Replacement roofs have included a new copper roof (1895) which was severely damaged in a storm and sold for scrap and a charcoaled tin roof (1914). In the most recent renovation (shown here, 1983), the roofs over the courtyard were refitted with precast concrete tiles placed into the original framework. These were covered with roofing paper and terne-coated stainless steel which was later painted the color of oxidized copper.

The Interior

Vestibules

Four vestibules connect the entrances with the inner corridors. The north and south are more imposing, with pendentive domed ceilings supported by arches that rest on cast-iron columns. The walls are embellished with semicircular niches, pressed-brick pilasters, and a decorative brick cornice. The less ornate east and west vestibules are barrel vaulted. They feature dentil cornices and semicircular niches between pairs of buff-colored pressed-brick pilasters that contrast with the red-brick walls and cornice.

In 1887 Meigs decorated the north and south vestibules with an elaborate and expensive scheme. In his Daily Memorandum of 3 March 1887, Meigs described the work as consisting of "painted architectural panels in Chiaro Oscuro with a little gilding in crown of the Pendentive domes." The cast-iron columns of the vestibules were bronzed using bronze powder in a gold-color paint. The north, south, and west vestibules served pedestrian traffic to the offices and had tiled floors similar to those of the corridors and Great Hall. The present terrazzo flooring was added after 1912. The east vestibule was for deliveries, and Meigs ordered installation of an "asphaltic-concrete" wagon track with cut-stone curbs extending into the southeast corner of the Great Hall to enable wagons to enter the building to deliver mail and supplies.

Great Hall

The Great Hall, 116 by 316 feet, is the most important feature of the building. It is divided into three courts by two screens of four colossal Corinthian columns which support the central roof. Each solid masonry column rises 75 feet, is constructed of 70,000 bricks, rests on a base 8 feet in diameter, and is crowned with a molded plaster capital and an abacus of cast iron weighing 3,200 pounds. The terra-cotta bases display a rich variety of decorative moldings.

Meigs was influenced by famous columns that he had seen or read about. In reference to the church of Santa Maria degli Angeli, Rome, converted by Michelangelo in 1563 from the tepidarium of the Baths of Diocletian (AD 302), he wrote: ". . . I found the inspiration which ruled much of the design of the great hall of my Pension Building here. The columns are of the same order but even exceed the Roman's in magnitude and height." He is also thought to have checked the dimensions of the great columns of the Temple of Jupiter at Baalbeck (sixty-five feet high and seven feet in diameter) and to have made sure that his were larger.

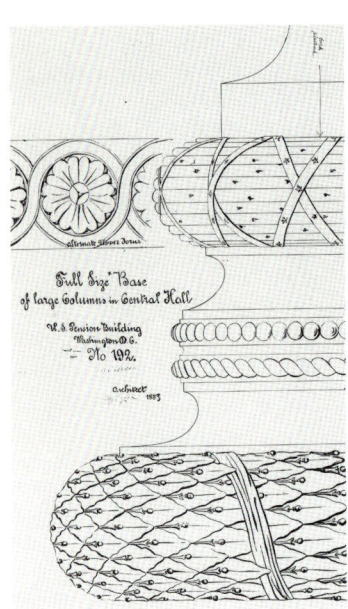

The terra-cotta bases of the Great Hall columns are embellished with (bottom to top) decorative laurel leaf garland, cable, bead, and fasces (or alternate patera) moldings, as ordered by Meigs in 1883.

34

Great Hall of the Pension Building.

Although the colossal columns were out of scale with those of the surrounding arcades, Meigs paid careful attention to the proportions of the columns themselves. As he refined the designs for the capitals of the columns, Meigs consulted the 1592 treatise on Roman architecture by the Italian architect Vignola.

For these magnificent columns of the Great Hall, Meigs envisioned a marble finish. However, for lack of funds, their plastered surfaces were given only a preliminary finish of white paint. It was not until 1895, three years after Meigs's death, that the columns and pilasters were painted to resemble Siena marble, and they appear in this condition in photographs as late as 1926. However, they were repainted in a single color at least by 1950, according to an undated clipping that reported spray painting with "4000 gallons of rose tan paint." The marbleizing of the columns was recreated in 1984, and, at the same time, the capitals were rebronzed. In addition, the bases were returned to their original finish of unpainted brick-colored terra cotta by the arduous removal of many layers of paint.

The central section of the Great Hall, 116 feet on each side, is the largest of the three. Its gabled roof rests on slender iron trusses and is 159 feet high at its peak. The lower side roofs rest on similar trusses which run perpendicular to those of the central section. The side roofs are surmounted by raised lanterns which provide additional light and ventilation. The windows of the lanterns are flanked by small spiral columns. The paint scheme seen in the lanterns today—including vermillion, cobalt, and bronze paint—is based on

This early photograph, ca. 1890, shows the presence of filing cabinets in west bay of the Great Hall. The colossal columns are not yet painted, but busts, urns, and gaslight fixtures are in place. Note also the original configuration of the fountain.

The renovation work in 1984 recreated the marbleizing of the colossal columns, not seen in photographs since 1926. Meigs planned to use the golden tones of Siena marble.

colors known to have been used in painting the lanterns in 1887 under Meigs's supervision.

An appropriation of 1894 permitted installation of a corrugated metal ceiling. The present roof is made of precast concrete tiles that are similar in appearance to the original terracotta tiles and double as the ceiling, painted sky blue as the metal ceiling was originally.

Above the fourth floor are several tiers of clerestory windows. The lowest tier is arcaded around the entire courtyard and is the one originally opened for ventilation of the building by employees who walked along the perimeter roof to do so. Above these, in the central bay on the north and south walls, are seven large arched windows, flanked by single pilasters, and above them, eleven smaller arched windows of graduated sizes. Also in the central bay on the east and west walls are five arched semicircular niches, flanked by paired pilasters, which echo the large arched windows of the north and south walls. Meigs may have arrived at this complex design to give greater prominence to the upper walls and cornice and thereby compensate for the plainness of roof and ceiling as dictated by cost.

Busts

In the cornice of the center bay is a band of 244 niches, each approximately two and one-half feet high, containing life-size busts, intended by Meigs to introduce "a variety of forms, lines and shadows" in the hall. In October 1886, while considering the idea of filling the niches with statuettes of military figures, he had busts of Carbulo (a Roman

Meigs's original plan to highlight the cornice of the center bay of the Great Hall with white plaster busts in dark niches was recreated in 1984.

Since the original nineteenth-century busts could not be found, the National Building Museum commissioned idealized sculptures symbolizing Americans who created our built environment.

general), Alexander Hamilton, and Sir Walter Scott placed there. Pleased with the effect, he asked the Smithsonian Institution "to make casts of some of the Ethnological heads, Savage & Civilized, to fill and give variety to the small niches."

Casts were made from molds of American Indians lent by the Smithsonian, and all were put in place by the end of the year, along with four more busts that were not part of the ethnological series—of Meigs himself, his father, and his wife, as well as one of Senator John Slidell of Louisiana. Only after the installations were well under way did Meigs learn that some of the molds were of federal prisoners, including convicted murderers; the rest were boys and girls from the Hampton Indian School.

The records of the heads were sealed in metal boxes to be stored in one of the niches, and presumably they remained in place with the original busts until the early-twentieth century. Photographs indicate that the busts were no longer in the niches by 1923. Although a search for the original busts was conducted, none was ever found. To fill the void, the National Building Museum in 1984 commissioned portrait sculptor Gretta Bader to create a series of eight idealized busts symbolizing Americans who created the built environment of the United States. The multiple casts of eight imaginary likenesses include an eighteenth-century bricklayer, a nineteenth-century architect, and a twentieth-century construction worker in a hard hat. They recreate the original appearance of the upper cornice of the central hall and at the same time reflect the current use of the building as a museum of the building arts.

Floor

The floor of the Great Hall was originally five-eighths-inch-thick burnt clay tile on a three-quarter-inch setting bed supported by three to four inches of rough concrete. Below this is six to ten inches of controlled fill which rests on the original soil of the site. The choice of clay tiles, widely used in public buildings, was discussed in Meigs's annual report of 1885. He noted that traffic was so heavy in the public areas of the building that wooden floors would not hold up; moreover, there was a need to wash these floors easily. Funds were appropriated in 1886, and the tiles that were installed were the specified "six-inch octagon tiles, with squares in their corners, in solid plain colors—gray, drab, and chocolate brown." These were made by the American Encaustic Tile Company of Zanesville, Ohio, and were laid in a pattern similar to that seen today inside the fountain and in the second-floor corridor.

Over the years, as office cubicles spread across the Great Hall, layers of asbestos or asphalt tile were laid over the tile floor. In 1972 the cubicles were removed, damaged areas filled in, and carpeting was installed with adhesive. This was replaced in 1985. In 1987 all remaining tiles were removed for storage and reuse, and the present carpet, designed for the Great Hall, was installed.

Fountain

The focal point of the courtyard is a large circular fountain, twenty-eight feet in diameter. It does not appear on the plans, but in August 1886 Meigs was known to be working on a drawing for a fountain with a rim or curb decorated with terra cotta in harmony with the bases of the colossal columns. For the center of the basin, Meigs desired a decorative fountain, and he corresponded with a London terra-cotta company about a design that he liked. However, due to lack of funds, he seems to have settled for a single jet of water shooting from a pile of rocks, as seen in early photographs. As office cubicles took over the Great Hall, the fountain was covered with a wooden surface that was eventually carpeted along with the rest of the floor. When the wooden floor was removed in 1980, the basin and rim were intact, and Florida coral rocks were found within. Recently, the fountain was restored with a new pumping mechanism and simple jet.

Arcaded Galleries

The rectangular Great Hall is surrounded by two levels of open arcaded galleries, reminiscent of the Palazzo

Cancelleria in Rome. The arcade consists of a series of brick arches that spring from seventy-two terra-cotta Roman Doric columns on the ground floor and the same number of cast-iron Ionic columns on the second floor. There are squared brick compound piers at the corners of the hall. The ceilings of these galleries consist of repeated shallow brick barrel vaults springing from rolled-iron I-beams. These vaults support the concrete floors of the second and third levels which are paved with clay tiles. The brick paneled parapet walls on the second and third levels are topped with marble coping. On the third level, reproductions of the original terra-cotta urns rest on the copings.

In choosing to compose the arcaded galleries with Doric columns on the lower level and Ionic columns above, Meigs was following the design precedents of the Italian Renaissance. However, the choice of different materials for the two types of columns seems to have been dictated by cost. Both types were hollow, and Meigs proposed in 1883 that these would be excellent spaces for the preservation of important documents. He had in mind collections of information "as will be interesting to the historians or the antiquarians of the age when the ruins of this building . . . shall be opened to the curious." Among the papers enclosed in

This plaque at the west entrance to the Great Hall commemorates the official completion of the building in 1887 and is accompanied by a glazed tintype of Abraham Lincoln. A similar photograph of U.S. Grant is located at the east entrance.

A unique feature of the Great Hall floor is the presidential seal, rendered in tiles and installed prior to the inaugural ball of 1901. It can be seen between the giant Corinthian columns that separate the west and central courts. This is thought to be the only permanent presidential seal installed in a public building other than the White House, a reminder of the long association of this building with inaugural balls.

Meigs had intended to fill the urns with plants to both decorate the building and improve the environment of the Great Hall. He sought to obtain plants from the Commissioner of Public Buildings and Grounds for both the urns and the main floor of the Great Hall by insisting that the hall was still part of Judiciary Square. His request was denied and photographs show that the urns contained plants only during inaugural balls.

the columns was a collection of maps, reports, and records from the War Department and a copper facsimile of the Declaration of Independence. Evidence indicates that Meigs filled over twenty columns with documents by the time the galleries were completed in 1884. Neither documents nor the columns that contain them have been disturbed in the hundred-year history of the building.

Decoration of the arcaded galleries did not begin until 1886 when a few iron columns in the southwest corner, opposite the Pension Commissioner's Suite, were bronzed on a trial basis. The result was praised by both Meigs and the Commissioner, and all of the cast-iron columns of the second tier and the beams of the second-floor gallery were bronzed in 1887. The first-floor columns were left unpainted until some time between the inaugural balls of 1889 and 1893. In photographs of the latter date, they appear dark in color, and recent paint analysis has revealed that the paint color at that time must have been a medium red, possibly marbleized, although they were later bronzed.

The plaster finish of the arcaded gallery walls was left unpainted for reasons of cost. By 1893, a forty-two-inch-high

This view of the third-floor corridor, taken in 1975, shows the distinctive pattern of floor tiles at that level. Note the absence of urns on the parapet, the assortment of inappropriate electric light fixtures, and the plain color scheme of the colossal columns.

decorative wainscotting with a marbleized pattern on a dark red ground was applied. This appears in early photographs and is confirmed by paint analysis. The sides of the parapets that face the Great Hall were also left unpainted at first, but paint analysis has shown early application of a light brown and yellow color scheme. Later in the twentieth century most of these decorative finishes were painted over with plain colors, and it was not until renovation work began in 1984 that any of these decorative finishes were reinstated. Also replaced were wooden spindle corner guards (where walls come together) which had been in place a long time but were probably not part of the original construction.

Originally, the Great Hall was artificially illuminated by gas sconces shaped like human arms above each column of the arcade. These remained in place until about 1900. Meigs had investigated the cost of electric lights, which were temporarily installed during construction and for inaugural balls, and recommended in 1885 that the Great Hall have electric arc lighting. However, due to expense, permanent electric lighting was not installed in the building until later. In 1984, single incandescent light bulbs were placed in the original locations of the first decorative gas fixtures.

Urns

The crowning detail of the arcaded galleries is the set of seventy-six urns on the third-floor parapet. Meigs considered the urns to be a very important part of the overall scheme, and their design was developed with great care. Not finding what he wanted in catalogs, Meigs created his own version of a shallow fluted bowl on a pedestal with a pair of eagle's head escutcheons on opposing sides. Historic photographs indicate that the terra-cotta urns were removed from the building by 1900.

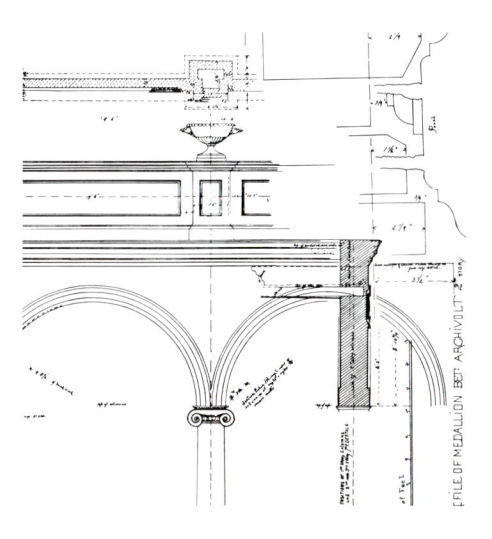

This drawing from Meigs's office shows that the design of the decorative urns on the third-floor parapet was developed with careful consideration for their location and appearance.

The fourth-floor balcony and document track are notable features of the Great Hall. The balcony, like the fourth floor itself, was added to the design during construction; its style is less inspired by classical precedents than other elements.

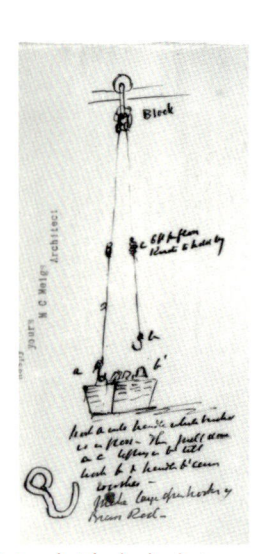

Meigs sketched a basket suspended from a trolley or wheel that moved on the document tracks to transport papers conveniently throughout the building. He noted in November 1887 that the lower track moved "over a ton of documents in the course of the working hours of the day."

The National Building Museum was able to find one of the original urns in the front yard of a house near the U. S. Soldiers' and Airmen's Home of Washington, DC, having been sent to that institution by a descendant of Meigs who remembered seeing such an urn there as a child. The owners of the house were happy to allow the urn to be copied, and thus the urns currently in place are exact plaster replicas of the originals.

Balcony and Document Track

A five-foot-wide balcony of wrought iron provides access to rooms on the fourth floor. The wood flooring rests on rolled-iron beams anchored in the brick wall and supported by wrought-iron brackets. The elegant original wrought-iron railing, repainted in gold, remains in place, although it is now supplemented by a higher inner rail for safety.

Above the balcony, a metal document track supported by ornate metal wall brackets extends around the perimeter of the Great Hall. On it originally traveled a trolley or wheel from which was suspended a basket that could hold 125 pounds of papers. Meigs installed one on each floor to facilitate the movement of documents around the building. In the northwest corner of the Great Hall is the shaft of a hand elevator,

The main stairs of the Pension Building are well known for their deep treads and shallow risers and unusual brick construction.

or dumbwaiter, for the purpose of moving papers vertically. The shaft and some of the elevator equipment remain intact but are now hidden behind a drywall installation.

Stairs and Elevators

The four main stairways of the Pension Building are centrally located on each side of the building near the entrances and extend from the first to the third floor. Their ceilings are barrel vaulted between the first and second floors to support the stairs above, groin vaulted at the first landings, and spanned by two kinds of small domes between the second and third floors.

The stairs themselves are constructed of and paved with brick and have unusually deep treads and shallow risers. The stairways still have their original wooden side handrails supported on rosette brackets, and the twenty-four foot wide north and south stairways also have central wood-and-iron railings that approximate the appearance of original ones, long since removed. The stairways were designed to be climbed easily by "the clerks and others in the Pension Bureau [who] are veteran soldiers or sailors, many of them more or less disabled after a four years' war."

Stairways to the fourth floor have their original ornate cherrywood balustrades, recently refinished.

Meigs had further intended to provide two hydraulic elevators for the wounded veterans near the north and south entrances and constructed the shafts for them. However, he could not obtain funds for the elevators, although the elevators that were later installed were placed in the shafts provided, as are the elevators installed in the current renovation.

Additional brick stairs on the east and west provide access to the fourth-floor balcony. These are placed in what would have been third-floor rooms before the plan of the building was altered to provide a fourth floor. These unusual stairs are graced with their original ornate cherrywood balustrades featuring elaborate newel posts and spiral balusters. Three additional stairways lead to the basement, and there is one to the roof.

The upper areas of the main stairways were decorated during the recent renovation to evoke the feeling of an original scheme executed under Meigs's supervision. Note the cast panel of the exterior frieze, one of several installed by Meigs in the stairways.

The upper areas of the main stairways were decorated under Meigs's personal supervision. He wrote in 1886 that "The hemispherical domes and the pendentives will need some lines in color and shade to bring out the forms satisfactorily." Around 1895, a painted red wainscotting was applied in all stairways, possibly to provide a finish more resistant to soiling in heavily used areas. Later in the twentieth century,

These typical second-floor office spaces with domed ceilings are connected by broad arches. They are currently used as temporary exhibition space.

most of these decorative finishes were painted over with pale colors, and it was not until renovation began in 1984 that some of these areas were redecorated to evoke their earlier appearance. The stairways also received new lighting at this time. The north, south, and west stairways are further decorated with selected cast panels of the exterior terra-cotta frieze of Civil War soldiers and sailors, placed there by Meigs so that they could be given closer inspection.

Offices

The office spaces around the perimeter of the Pension Building are typically twenty-six by thirty-seven feet with domed brick ceilings, twenty-four feet in diameter. The ceilings transfer their loads to elliptical arches located on all four sides of the rooms. Central ceiling height is eighteen feet on the first floor and twenty-two feet on the second. Groin-vaulted ceilings are found in all corner offices on these floors as well as the rooms directly behind the elevator shafts next to the north and south entrances. Barrel-vaulted ceilings are found in rooms next to the stairways. The third-floor offices have ceilings of shallow brick arches resting on rolled-iron I-beams at a height of nineteen feet. The fourth-floor storage rooms, lit by skylights, have sloping ceilings that vary in height from ten to fourteen feet and which were, at one time, lined with corrugated sheet metal to reduce heat accumulation in summer. Interior dividing walls are load-bearing brick masonry arches with nonbearing masonry infill.

Domes

The domed brick ceilings of the offices are especially interesting, because this form of structural support for floor systems is rarely found in the United States. All-masonry construction, fully developed by Roman times, was typical of monumental buildings of the early-nineteenth century and was the preferred method for fireproofing. This construction typically utilized combinations of solid bearing walls, column-and-lintel systems, and groin and barrel vaults. Meigs's decision to build the more complicated brick domes on pendentives is not fully understood, but he may have wanted to provide unusually elegant classical ceilings for the large office spaces.

Since workmen were unfamiliar with such domes, their construction had to be carefully supervised. Even the groin vaults, although more commonly used in the United States, required close attention, in part because Meigs chose to use a system for laying bricks that was common in Germany but not here.

Office Lighting

Simple gaslight fixtures were suspended from the center of the ceilings of the offices to supplement the daylight that was intended as the main lighting source. More elaborate chandeliers from the former pension offices were probably installed in the Pension Commissioner's Suite and other executive offices. The gas lighting was replaced with electricity sometime after 1896 and probably no later than 1913. The electric lighting was then replaced piecemeal until the current renovation which provides a uniform system of contemporary lighting designed to highlight the ceiling vaults while providing even illumination in workplaces and flexible lighting in exhibition galleries and public spaces.

The perimeter offices are amply supplied with daylight from large casement windows which originally opened into the rooms to promote airflow. All were double glazed, an unusual feature, to economize heat in winter, and most were equipped with awnings to provide relief from summer sun.

The windows were carefully designed, and specifications called for materials of high quality. They were replaced with double-hung windows after some were damaged by a storm in July 1913. During the current renovation, the office windows have been replaced with inoperable replicas of the original casements, in keeping with current standards for regulating the interior environment, which is now controlled by a computer-operated heating and air-conditioning system. A few windows on the first floor can be opened, however, to provide additional fire escape routes during inaugural balls and other high-density uses of the building.

The fourth-floor storage rooms are equipped with skylights which originally could be opened to provide ventilation. These were added to the design of the building after it was decided to divide the high-ceilinged third-floor offices to provide a floor for record storage. Two fourth-floor rooms adjacent to the east and west stairways originally housed steam-driven exhaust fans in large circular skylights intended to increase airflow through the building. All of the original skylight designs have been reproduced (without the fans) in the current renovation.

Floors

The floors of the offices are wood, with layers of tongue-and-groove flooring on wood joists. The joists span wood beams which are, in turn, supported by brick piers which rest on the masonry vault below. On the fourth floor, a concrete floor was poured over the brick arches and wrought-iron beams of the third-floor ceiling to produce the strongest floor in the building. Over the years, many of the wood floors on the lower levels were damaged and overlaid with asbestos or asphalt tile. During the recent renovation, it was necessary to work beneath many of the floors. Thereafter, only basic repairs were made, and all office spaces were carpeted for current use.

Doors

The doors of the office spaces represent an interesting history of installations in the Pension Building. For ventilation purposes, Meigs preferred that the offices not have doors, but over the years doors were installed piecemeal and did not conform to a single design. The first important installation took place in the Pension Commissioner's Suite in 1885. The wide arch connecting the anteroom to the adjacent deputy commissioner's office was bricked up so that the main suite could be isolated from other offices. Doors were installed between the rooms and at the entrances from the corridor, ac-

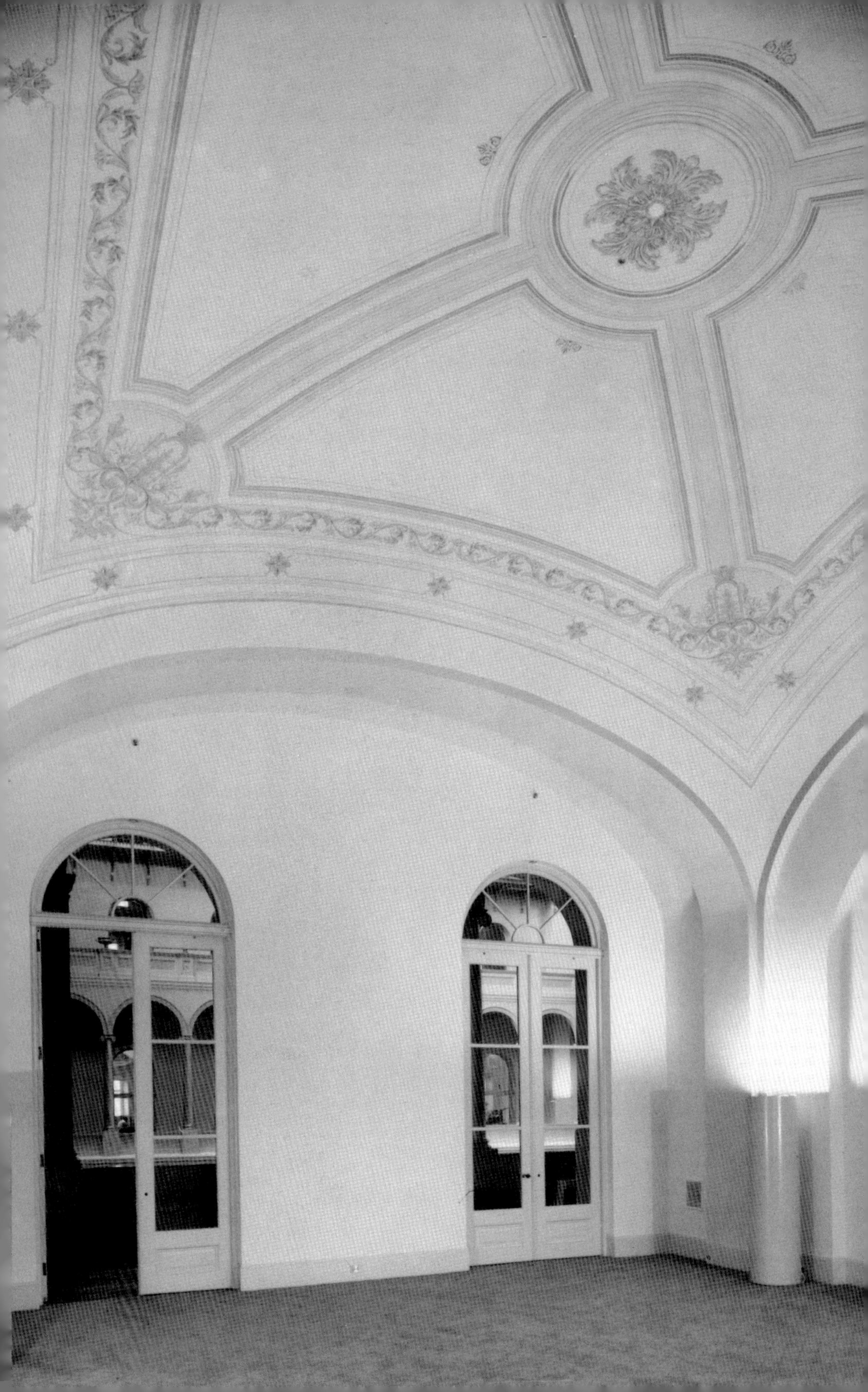

cording to an undated drawing, which provided guidance for the recent renovation of the suite. The adjacent offices of the deputy commissioners and chief clerk also received glass doors, some of which were "Venetian Blind Doors" to provide privacy. An additional room on the west side of the Pension Commissioner's Suite was walled off with bricks, the floor paved with concrete, and the entrances secured with iron doors to provide a vault for the large sums of cash handled by the bureau.

The other offices apparently remained without doors, although Meigs, noting that some clerks had hung old carpets in doorways on the third floor, would have installed them if he had had money in his budget in 1885. In budget requests of 1885 and 1892, money for doors was requested by the commissioner, and doors were eventually installed throughout the building, as were many partitions between and within offices. The current renovation has sought to return the office spaces to their original configurations by removing all partitions except those bricked in by the pension commissioner. With the exception of a small number of drywall panels, doorways that must be filled for purposes of climate control, security, or privacy are sealed with large expanses of glass or simple glass doors.

Pension Commissioner's Suite

Although many of the building's plaster surfaces were not painted until 1895, ornamental painted designs were executed earlier in selected areas, including executive offices. The Pension Commissioner's Suite was painted in 1885 in a combination of oil and water base paint. The domed ceilings were "to be in light tints; decoration in harmonious shades of different colors," while "darker, warm tints" were specified for the walls. In 1886, the ceilings of the adjacent deputy commissioners' and chief clerk's offices were also painted in watercolors or distemper under Meigs's supervision.

The only original decorated ceiling to have survived is that of the pension commissioner's anteroom. It was cleaned in 1984 with artist's erasers and gentle brushing. The small areas damaged by previous installation of fluorescent light fixtures were restored. The richly detailed design, characteristic of the late-nineteenth century, suggests the scheme that Meigs might have followed for the entire building if his budget had permitted. Of particular note is the illusionistic shadowing of the painted central medallion on the side away from the natural light of the windows. The color scheme of the rest of the room is not original.

This original painted ceiling in the anteroom of the Pension Commissioner's Suite is the only one to have survived throughout the building's one-hundred-year history. It was cleaned in 1984 with artist's erasers. The doors, which were installed at the same time, are reproductions of the originals.

Original fireplace in the Pension Commissioner's Suite.

The Pension Commissioner's Suite contains a large open-hearth fireplace on the south wall of the second room. This was added to the plans and constructed in 1885 of pressed brick with thin joints of tinted mortar and a lintel and carved brackets of Ohio sandstone. Set into the lintel are decorative glazed tiles depicting horsemen of the Parthenon frieze, a work of art much admired by Meigs and the inspiration for the building's exterior frieze of Civil War soldiers. A mantel and overmirror are found on the west wall of the commissioner's private office; this is thought to have been installed at a later date and is not mentioned in any historic documents.

The Pension Commissioner's Suite was also provided with a bathroom in the small corner room off the private office. This had a Minton tile floor, standard bath fixtures, and a steam-coil apparatus. Although plumbing and bathroom fixtures have always been located in this space, nothing of the original equipment remains, and the current renovation has converted this space into a kitchen. Toilet rooms for other employees and visitors were originally located on the first three floors next to the east and west stairways. All are now relocated, but some marble stalls from a 1912 renovation have been retained.

The Pension Bureau's mail-handling facilities in the Great Hall, photographed between 1912 and 1923. Note the original tile floor.

History in the Pension Building

For virtually all of its history, the Pension Building has been a government office building, just as it was intended to be. The Pension Bureau stayed until 1926 when it was merged with the Veterans Administration and moved to another location. The bureau used the building more or less as Meigs intended, although early photographs show temporary installation of files and mail-handling facilities in the Great Hall.

The building was then turned over to the General Accounting Office (GAO), a young but growing agency, which almost immediately began to place desks in the Great Hall, illuminated by light fixtures strung across the space at the first-floor level. This utilization of the Great Hall expanded steadily and even included placing files in the fountain which could be conveniently consulted while sitting on the rim. In 1934 it was proposed to clad the building's late-nineteenth-century facade with marble in the classical style, as well as to add wings at either end. This plan was not pursued, and GAO eventually built a new building across G Street and moved there in 1950.

The General Accounting Office placed desks in the Great Hall immediately after occupying the building in 1926.

By 1940, as this newspaper photograph shows, files were stored in the fountain of the Great Hall.

This 1967 Historic American Buildings Survey photograph shows the Great Hall fully occupied by office cubicles.

An information desk occupied the center of the carpeted Great Hall in 1975.

The Civil Service Commission became the next tenant until it moved to a new building in 1963. By this time, the floor of the Great Hall was fully occupied by ceilingless office partitions with banks of fluorescent lights. The fountain was covered with a wooden floor permitting office space on top. From 1972 to 1978 the Superior Court of the District of Columbia occupied the building while new quarters were being constructed nearby. Since the courts did not need so much office space, the partitions in the Great Hall were removed. The badly-damaged tile floor, including the wooden floor covering the fountain, was carpeted, and an information desk occupied the center of the Great Hall. Succeeding agencies continued to use the space in a similar manner until the National Building Museum was created in 1980 and work began to restore the building and adapt it to museum use.

This photograph of the pension commissioner in his private corner office in 1894 shows original windows, a gaslight fixture probably brought from an earlier office, an entrance to the vault hidden behind a bookcase and a curtain, and a wall-to-wall patterned carpet. The mantle and overmirror on the left (not a working fireplace) have a "firescreen" of a framed cast panel of the exterior frieze.

Inaugural Balls

A unique aspect of the history of the Pension Building is an association with inaugural balls that spans more than a century. The first inaugural balls were held for George Washington, in 1789 in New York and 1793 in Philadelphia. The next president to have an inaugural ball was James Madison in 1809, at Long's Hotel in Washington. Subsequent balls were held in hotels, assembly rooms, and theaters. As the size of the event grew, temporary pavilions were erected in Judiciary Square for Presidents Zachary Taylor (1849), James Buchanan (1857), Abraham Lincoln (1861), and Ulysses S. Grant (1873). At the 1873 event the temperature dropped to minus four degrees Fahrenheit and caged canaries that were part of the decorations froze. Subsequent balls took place indoors, moving to the Pension Building in 1885 for Grover Cleveland's first inaugural ball, even before construction was completed. A temporary wooden roof was erected over the open courtyard and a wooden floor laid over the dirt of the construction site. Elaborate decorations masked the unfinished interior; electric lights provided illumination.

Up to 1909 six more glittering balls were held in the Pension Building, for Presidents Benjamin Harrison, William McKinley, Theodore Roosevelt, and William Howard Taft, each inevitably described as the best ever. Each featured elaborate decorations, floral displays, and greenery to give the effect of an elegant conservatory. In all but one ball, a huge canopy of broad streamers hid the roof from view. Electric lighting, still a novelty, created dazzling effects. Famous bands played music for dancing and promenades; fine meals were served and huge crowds attended.

In 1913 Woodrow Wilson chose not to have a ball, and the custom of holding these events fell out of favor until after World War II. When the balls were restored to the inaugural agenda, they were held as multiple events at a variety of halls, but the Pension Building could no longer be used as a site because the Great Hall had been subdivided by office partitions. It wasn't until 1973, when the partitions were removed, that one of Richard Nixon's three inaugural balls was held at the Pension Building. Since then, one of the balls for each inaugural year has been held in the Great Hall for Presidents Jimmy Carter, Ronald Reagan, and George Bush. The setting for the balls of 1985 and 1989 was especially elegant, as the original appearance of the Great Hall had by then been restored.

Inaugural Balls

In all, twelve inaugural balls have been held in the Pension Building—seven between 1885 and 1909 and five since 1973.

1897, President William McKinley

1905, President Theodore Roosevelt

1901, President William McKinley

1989, President George Bush

Program, President William McKinley

Criticisms, Myths, and Ghost Stories

Among the aspects of history in the Pension Building are the criticisms, myths, and ghost stories associated with it. The building, although admired by some, was criticized even during construction for its unusual design and massive appearance, as well as its mounting costs. From an early time it seems to have had the nickname "Meigs's Old Red Barn," and this may be the source of a persistent myth, for which there is no verifiable evidence, that Meigs intended for horses to be stabled within the building, even on the fourth floor, traversing the brick stairs to get there. Another popular story is that a famous Civil War general, either William Tecumseh Sherman or Philip H. Sheridan, commented, "It's too bad the damn thing is fireproof."

In the twentieth century, John Clagett Procter, in his *Washington Past and Present*, (1930) wrote: "The building has served a useful purpose as an example to our national legislators of what not to do, and fortunately it is located in a not very prominent place." General Ulysses S. Grant III, who was actively involved in the city's development, described the building in 1944 as an architectural incongruity, although he later changed his mind and was pleased when the building was recommended for preservation.

Ghost stories have long been associated with the building. Many figures have been seen to come and go in the marbleizing of the colossal Corinthian columns, especially at night when not too many people are around. One of these stories is associated with William F. Cody ("Buffalo Bill") who attended at least one of the early inaugural balls. Ghostly figures have been said to appear in the corridors and stairways, both on horseback and on foot. One was reported to have a distinctive limp and is thought to be associated with James Tanner, a pension commissioner who lost both feet in the Second Battle of Bull Run.

Renovation of the central section of the Great Hall, 1984.

Renovation and Contemporary Use

Once the General Accounting Office relocated in 1950, the Pension Building began to be considered obsolete. While contemplating the option of demolition, the General Services Administration commissioned a report by architect Chloethiel Woodard Smith to explore other possibilities for the building's use. This report, issued in 1967 and entitled "The Pension Building: A Building in Search of a Client," first introduced the concept that the building be converted to a museum of the building arts. This proposal eventually led to the formation in 1975 of a Committee for the Museum of the Building Arts which worked toward the goal of saving the building and creating the museum. In 1978 Congress passed a resolution calling for the preservation of the building as a national treasure, and in 1980, passed legislation mandating the creation of the National Building Museum and establishing a public-private partnership between the General Services Administration, the Department of the Interior, and the museum. Under the terms of this partnership, the federal government makes the Pension Building available, without charge, as the museum's home, while the museum, as a private foundation, looks primarily to the private sector for support of its programs. The museum has used the Pension building since 1980, conducting tours and other educational programs and issuing publications even before its first exhibitions opened to the public in October 1985.

Restoration and renovation of the building proceeded under the supervision and control of the General Services Administration, which acts as "landlord" for the federal government. As a first step, Cooper-Lecky Architects were engaged in 1981–83 to conduct preliminary planning and design the replacement of the roof over the Great Hall. Next, the architectural firm of Keyes Condon Florance (with Giorgio Cavaglieri as associate architect) was retained to provide full-scale design for renovation and adaptive reuse of the building. The contractors were Grunley-Walsh Construction Co., Inc. and NICO, Inc.

The first phase of the renovation, commencing in 1984, included redecoration of the Great Hall (to evoke its original nineteenth-century appearance in time for the 1985 inaugural ball), cleaning the building's exterior, providing temporary gallery space and conference facilities for the National Building Museum, and renovating the Pension Commissioner's Suite. Later phases have included structural renovation of the building, with replacement and upgrading of all utilities, and the provision of permanent facilities for the National Building Museum on the first two floors and general-purpose office space on the third and fourth floors.

The National Building Museum presents exhibits in galleries installed in the former office spaces of the Pension Building and in the Great Hall.

Sheet Metal Craftsmanship: Progress in Building, 1988

Epilogue

The National Building Museum is a privately-funded institution operating under a Congressional mandate to celebrate American achievements in building and to encourage excellence in the building arts. To fulfill this mandate, the museum conducts a wide range of programs for both the general public and special groups.

Anatomy of A Bridge: Seven Steps in Constructing the Brooklyn Bridge, 1985–1986

In the museum galleries, permanent and temporary exhibitions interpret the world of architecture and engineering, urban planning, historic preservation, construction techniques, and building trades. The museum also circulates such exhibitions to community and university museums across the country.

The museum offers educational programs for all ages and interests that include classes for students, elementary through high school; and tours of the Pension Building, its environs, and to construction and building sites of unusual interest. An annual Festival of the Building Arts brings together skilled artisans to demonstrate and explain crafts ranging from masonry to gilding.

Publications include brochures, posters, and catalogues relating to exhibitions and educational programs, as well as a quarterly journal, BLUEPRINTS.

The museum's collection comprises works on paper—photographs and drawings—and architectural models and artifacts. Materials on the construction and use of the Pension Building are particularly strong.

The majestic Great Hall, historically the site of presidential inaugural balls, is available by special membership to cultural organizations, corporations, and associations for private use.

The museum's annual Festival of the Building Arts enables skilled artisans to share historic and contemporary crafts with visitors.

Glossary

abacus	flat slab on the top of the capital of a column
arcaded gallery	covered passageway with openings through a series of arches supported by columns
balustrade	railing supported by a series of small posts or balusters
barrel vault	masonry ceiling of semicylindrical shape supported by parallel walls or arcades
belt course	horizontal band on the facade of a building, usually defining the interior floor levels
capital	topmost feature of a column or pilaster
clerestory	elevated series of windows in a wall that rises above adjoining roofs
console	ornamental bracket in the form of a vertical scroll serving as a support
coping	protective cap or cover on top of a wall
corbelling	parallel masonry layers, each projecting beyond the one below in step-like fashion
Corinthian column	having a capital decorated with stylized acanthus leaves and small scrolls or volutes (see drawing, p. 35)
cornice	projecting ornamental molding along the top of a building or wall
dentil	one of an ornamental band of small rectangular tooth-like blocks
Doric column	having a plain capital (see drawing, p. 35) (Doric columns of the Pension Building are **Roman Doric,** having bases and unfluted shafts)
frieze	horizontal ornamental band, often in relief
gable roof	double-sloping or pitched roof
groin vault	masonry ceiling formed by two intersecting barrel vaults of identical shape
Ionic column	having a capital decorated with prominent scrolls or volutes (see drawing, p. 35)
keystone	central wedge-shaped stone of an arch
lantern	windowed superstructure crowning a roof or dome (long rectangular lanterns of the Pension Building resemble **monitors** of nineteenth-century factories)
lintel	horizontal structural element that spans an opening
modillion	scroll-shaped bracket used in series under a cornice

parapet	low wall along the edge of a roof or balcony
pediment	ornamental surface element, above a door or window, usually triangular but can also be rounded
pendentive	concave triangular area of wall at each corner of a domed space which provides transition between supporting walls or arches and the dome above
pier	solid masonry support, usually square or rectangular
pilaster	shallow pier attached to a wall, often decorated to resemble a classical column
pressed brick	brick formed under hydraulic pressure that has a smooth hard surface and precisely uniform shape
Roman Doric	see Doric
running bond	pattern in which bricks are laid end to end
sidelight	framed area of fixed glass alongside a door or window
spandrel	roughly triangular space between the exterior curve of an arch and the surrounding framework
terra cotta	fine-grained hard-fired clay used for decoration, roof tiles, and fireproofing; literally "cooked earth"
truss	rigid framework made of small triangular elements and designed to span an opening
vault	arched masonry ceiling